Successful Leadership Book For Families

Have an Amazing Family By Applying 15 Successful Tried & True Corporate Tools

Every year corporations spend thousands of dollars developing ways to keep their employees happy, motivated, creative and high-functioning.

In this revolutionary Itty Bitty Book, Jacqueline T. D. Huynh shows you how to use these same corporate techniques to create a happy dynamic family.

Introduce and nurture these simple but important 15 ideas within your family structure and you will instill and promote the exact corporate skills for your family to become your own winning team at home.

For example:

- Discuss and decide core values for your family.
- Create a family culture that promotes laughter, support, joy and communication.
- Create a high level of emotional intelligence, respectful expression and compassion.

Pick up a copy of this powerful book today and experience the joys and successes that come when you invest in creating a loving, close family.

Reviews

"Jacqueline T.D. Huynh (Schaeffer) is my life guru. Her wisdom and gentle guidance approach is sensible with amazing clarity and depth. This book condenses an enormously complex topic into bite size pieces. The reader will gain much needed support, insight, specific and helpful advice. A wonderful companion…I don't leave home without it!"

~ Amazon Customer

"The beauty of this book is its simple common sense. It is clear that Ms. Huynh (Schaeffer) has been able to acquire skills that qualify her to guide others into more constructive living. Her bio states: "She helps business owners and families develop skills to become successful leaders in order to manifest their vision and leave a legacy."

~ Amazon Customer

"Most importantly, Jacqueline T. D. Huynh (Schaeffer), herself, possesses skills which more than qualify her to offer a method of working with families that courts successful outcomes verified via client feedback and fosters better family functioning. Can you think of anything more important as we advance technologically? She will explain to you that technology is here to stay, so finding a way to bring back improved communications among family members despite the prevalence of technology in our lives is a critical focus for all parents and children."

~ Burton N. Danet, Ph.D.

Your Amazing Itty Bitty® Family Leadership Book

15 Simple Tips Successful Companies Use That Parents Can Implement At Home

Jacqueline T. D. Huynh

Published by Itty Bitty® Publishing
A subsidiary of S & P Productions, Inc.

Copyright © 2016 Jacqueline T. D. Huynh

All rights reserved. No part of this book may be reproduced or transmitted in any form or by any means, electronic or mechanical, including photocopying, recording or by any information storage and retrieval system, without written permission of the publisher, except for inclusion of brief quotations in a review.

Printed in the United States of America

Itty Bitty® Publishing
311 Main Street, Suite E
El Segundo, CA 90245
(310) 640-8885

ISBN: 978-1-931191-10-4

This is dedicated to my beautiful and loving children, Ava-Loann and Alex-Minh, who will forever be my inspiration, students and teachers. I'm thankful to be a part of their life journey and blessed they have chosen me to be their mother.

In memory of Tina, my beloved sister. You are missed and loved.

To my wonderful parents, Loc and Lana Huynh, and my sisters, Denice, Leesa, Michelle, my extended family and fabulous friends for their continued love and support.

And for the guidance of my amazing mentors, Keith Miller, John Lovejoy and Dan Nance who have been instrumental in my journey of self-growth, self-discovery and life path.

Stop by our Itty Bitty® website to find interesting blog entries regarding Successful Leadership Techniques.

www.IttyBittyPublishing.com

Or

Visit my website at www.IntegrativeMinds.com

Table of Contents

Tip 1.		Having Leadership is Important
Tip 2.		Creating Core Values
Tip 3.		Having a Vision Statement
Tip 4.		Stating Your Mission
Tip 5.		Fostering a Positive Culture
Tip 6.		Setting Goals Successfully
Tip 7.		Knowing Strengths and Blind Spots
Tip 8.		Developing Effective Communication
Tip 9.		Encouraging Motivation and Engagement
Tip 10.		Showing Compassion
Tip 11.		Improving Emotional Intelligence
Tip 12.		Listening Actively
Tip 13.		Forming Powerful Alliances
Tip 14.		Tapping Into Intuition
Tip 15.		Leading by Example

Introduction

Successful companies like Google, Zappos and Apple set short- and long-term goals and have metrics that measure success that are agreed upon by key players including management and employees.

But, many families today are simply in survival mode; they are trying to catch their breath as they get through the hectic schedules of the day, of the week. Many families don't share dinner or communicate. This and the lack of planning lead to a constant state of flux and frustration as family members are at odds with each other.

Happy family, however, are at peace and have the ability to navigate conflict among themselves as they exercise emotional intelligence; they feel they are working toward shared goals as they discuss values and mission; children become independent adults.

It is the book's goal that your family can benefit from using the strategies that successful companies already adopt from millions of dollars spent on business coaching and consulting. We hope that you will instill this blueprint and lead a more harmonious life with your loved ones.

Leadership

Tip #1
Having Leadership is Important

The top-earning companies consistently have the highest employee satisfaction ratings every year. These employees say the main reasons are because they have great bosses/leaders.

A leader is someone who guides and directs. The attributes of a great boss/leader are the following.

1. Inspires their employees.
2. Motivates & empowers everyone to contribute at full potential.
3. Shows respect and compassion.
4. Leads by example.
5. Empathizes and sympathizes.
6. Listens actively and acts decisively.
7. Gives others a chance to shine.
8. Knows when to lead in front or step back.
9. Has control of his/her emotions.
10. Serves as a mentor, coach and teacher.

Why is Leadership Important as a Parent?

Parents are the epicenter to the support and success of the family. Begin thinking of yourself as a leader of your family. You are the Leader of your family. Implement skills and strategies employed by successful CEO's who operate world-class companies. Some of the primary benefits to your family are the following:

- Improved sense of self-worth.
- Increased self-reliance.
- Being more responsive to one another.
- Accepting greater responsibilities.
- Increased confidence.
- Stress reduction.
- Excellent judgment skills.
- Stable & happy life.
- More successful and fulfilling career.
- Loving and honest relationships.
- Working harder and smarter.
- Living in generosity & integrity.
- Setting, obtaining and sustaining goals.
- Healthy work life balance.
- Healing space.
- Awesome happy family! ☺

Tip #2
Creating Core Values

"Values" are the principles that guide organizations' conduct, how they perform their work and how they interact with others. Values underpin beliefs and priorities. Understanding employee's values can provide insight into creating high engagement culture and improved performance.

Values:

1. Are hidden drivers of human behavior and also known as guiding principles.
2. Encompass who you are and what you believe in.
3. Reflects your identity and strength.
4. Are the reasons you make a decision to do or not do something.
5. Are the key to unleashing creativity, innovation and passion.
6. Are the source of unhappiness if they have been violated.
7. Are where the most conflict happens if they are different.
8. Are how we prioritize our time, energy and money.
9. Are how we make decisions about our life.

How to Create Your Family's Core Values

First, get all family members together to answer the following questions. This is an important exercise, so BE sure to write down the answers!

- Identify times when you were each the happiest, most proud and most satisfied. Ask yourself what needs or desires were being fulfilled.
- Identify 3-5 traits that you would like to pass on to your children.
- Think of two people you admire and list two words to describe each of them.
- What are two principles you would be willing to fight for?
- Describe yourself in one word.
- What two rules should everyone follow in life?
- Designate your top five core values.

Share all your answers and have a discussion. Why is it important? Define what it looks like and what it doesn't look like. Define success.

Now together create <u>your</u> top five core values for the family and agree to live by them.

Agree about a reward system based on family members living up to the core values.

Tip #3
Having a Vision Statement

A Vision Statement is an image of where the company wants to be in the future. The key is how they want to be remembered and what impact they created.

1. A clear vision helps employees focus on what's important and how their contribution is helping the long-term goal.
2. The statement is inspirational and motivational.
3. The vision statement of Feeding America is *"A hunger-free America."*
4. The vision statement of Google is *"To provide access to the world's information in one click."*
5. The vision statement of Amazon is *"To be earth's most customer centric company; to build a place where people can come to find and discover anything they might want to buy online."*
6. Vision statements can be short or long.
7. What kind of legacy will you leave to the next generation?

How to Create Your Family's Vision Statement

- This is the statement that expresses the hopes and dreams for your family.
- It also puts an intention to the future.
- Get your family together to brainstorm.
- Use this time to <u>really</u> listen and connect with your family.
- Have each person talk about what he/she wants the family to achieve....the life's dream (dream big).
- Keep in mind your 5 core values.
- Create a short & simple statement that captures this dream.
- Everyone votes to agree on the statement.
- This will give everyone a sense that they are important, special and contributing to the family.
- A sample vision statement is, *"To ensure and support every family member in achieving his/her fullest potential while living in health, love and abundance."*
- Another sample vision statement is, *"For every family member to contribute to all aspects of life and create opportunities for themselves and others."*

Tip #4
Stating Your Mission

A Mission Statement defines the purpose, goals and standard of the company. It's the reason for existing.

1. It is what the company does, whom they do it for and how they do it.
2. It states what are the benefits.
3. A clear Mission Statement helps employees understand operations, decisions and changes.
4. It helps with planning and achieving engagement around a common goal.
5. The mission statement for Google is *"To organize the world's information and make it universally accessible and useful."*
6. The mission statement for Ikea is, *"So together, we save money for a better everyday life."*
7. The mission statement for Habitat for Humanity is, *"Seeking to put God's love into action, Habitat for Humanity brings people together to build homes, communities and hope."*

How to Create Your Family's Mission Statement

- This is how memories are created.
- Get your family together to brainstorm.
- Use this time to really listen and connect with your family.
- Each person talk about what they see the family being like.
- Each person shares the steps in getting there.
- Each person explains why they want to get there.
- Keep in mind your five core values.
- Create a short & simple statement that captures this goal.
- Everyone votes to agree.
- This will give everyone a sense that they are important, special and contributing to the family.
- Refer to your Mission Statement often.
- A sample mission statement is, *"To love, help and believe in each other. To use our time, skills, and assets to be of service for others."*
- Another sample mission statement is, *"To foster individuality and communication while supporting the growth of new ideas, thoughts and dreams for each family member."*

Tip #5
Fostering a Positive Culture

Corporate Culture makes up the shared values, beliefs and behaviors that determine how a company's employees and management think, feel and act. Google does this by creating a work environment that attracts, motivates and retains the best employees.

1. A company's culture could be the dress code, employee benefits, perks, flex time, on-site childcare, massages or gym.
2. A healthy corporate culture values each and every employee. A few examples: Backing them up with clients, making time for them, and showing a genuine interest in their ideas and aspirations.
3. This result is employees working as a team towards the company's mission, vision and goals.
4. Employees have positive attitudes and are loyal when they are being rewarded for their contributions and acknowledged as assets to the company.
5. There is a reduction in turnover.
6. There is a reduction in sickness.
7. It improves the productivity of a business, thereby creating more revenues.

How to Create a Positive Family Culture

Every family has a culture…mostly by default. Now create one by design with daily investment. Think of a happy family with loved ones hanging out at their house:

- What was it like? A great atmosphere? Happy parents? Fun things to do? Are there lots of love, respect and support? How are these things demonstrated? How does it feel?
- Connect these things to your immediate family.
- Keep in mind your five core values by constantly reinforcing them.
- Teach one another and lead by example.
- Create rituals and traditions while keeping all these things in mind.
- Continue to read and learn about how your children change during each stage of development as well as your spouse so you can understand how each person affects the family dynamic.
- A great guide book to help your teenagers prepare for success, as an adult is, ***"Conversations with the Wise Aunt/Uncle" * by Dennis E. Coates**

Tip #6
Setting Goals Successfully

In the corporate community, successful businesses know the value of setting realistic goals tied into rewards at milestones and celebrations at completion.

A tried and true method commonly used for goals is known as the S.M.A.R.T. Method.

1. **S**pecific & Simple: Write a short sentence stating specifically what you want. What specific steps do you need to take?
2. **M**easurable & Meaningful: How will you know when you've achieved the goal? Why do you want to achieve the goal?
3. **A**chievable: Is it possible to achieve?
4. **R**easonable and Responsible: What could get in the way? What will you gain/lose? Is it good for you, for others and for the world?
5. **T**ime-Oriented: State the time/day/month/year when it will be completed.

Goal Setting For The Family

When it comes to goal setting for the family, it's important to include all family members in the process of setting the goals and time frame of completion.

- Get all family members together.
- Remember all goals need to be written down.
- Use the corporate S.M.A.R.T. format and adapt it to your family in a fun way.
- Talk about the vision or desired end results.
- Discuss the requirements to achieve the goal and who will accomplish which tasks.
- Assist everyone with focusing on the specific steps to complete the goals.
- Create a feeling of "we're all in this together" because this improves the chances of engagement and "buy-in".
- Be sure to celebrate at milestone and at completion. Make it fun along the way.
- This is about the journey as well as the destination.

Tip #7
Knowing Strengths and Blind Spots

"Enter every activity without giving mental recognition to the possibility of defeat. Concentrate on your strengths, instead of your weaknesses... on your powers, instead of your problems."
- Paul Meyers

In business it's important to know your strengths and blind spots (weaknesses) for the following reasons:

1. Knowing your strengths will save you time.
2. It will help you grow faster.
3. Give you a sense of purpose.
4. Which will boost your confidence and increase your odds of succeeding, and that will make you happy.
5. Knowing your blind spots will help you create a more effective team structure.
6. It will also help you bring in people who have complimentary skills.
7. Having achieved #5 and #6, it will reduce stress and increase performance.

How to See Strengths and Blind Spots

- Encourage your children and partner to participate in activities that resonate with their heart's desire.
- Support your children and partner in the pursuit of their dream and the profession they choose.
- Avoid projecting your expectations or your dreams in your children's life. This is particularly important to the "Tiger Moms" and "Stage Moms."
- Help your family members see their blind spots, find their strengths and identify what they are good at doing.
- Coach your children and lead them!
- Ask open-ended questions about how they feel and think.
- Discuss and share positive things.
- Again, ask them how they feel and think.
- Adjust your positions as necessary.
- Keep matching them and asking them.
- Step back and allow them to make the mistakes and learn the lessons gently.
- Teach them how to adjust themselves through leading by example.
- Champion and be a support for whatever the outcome as you grow together.

Tip #8
Developing Effective Communication

Effective communication begins with listening and observing, then acknowledging and validating and finally, powerful questions.

Because:

1. Employees want leaders who are accessible; who not only talk but listen.
2. They want to know what they offer makes a difference to the company.
3. They want to be acknowledged, valued and respected for their contribution.
4. They want to be a part of the processes and participate in decisions that affect their role.
5. They want training, development and opportunities for advancement, because it shows the company cares.
6. When they feel the company cares, they work harder.

How to be an Effective Communicating Parent

- Create consistent family meals together … at least five times a week.
- Each person can share what was great about the day, what was not and how could it be better.
- Share what each of you is thankful for.
- Cement the five core values again.
- Strengthen the family bond.
- Create feelings of nurturing support.
- Statistics show how communication decreases obesity, depression, teen pregnancy, crimes and drug use.
- Effective communication increases the potential for well-adjusted children.
- During tough times, communicate more.
- Learn how your children communicate and adjust to their needs accordingly.
- Communicate in a calm, cool and collected manner. To learn more effective ways of yelling less and loving more go to **www.TheOrangeRhino.com.**
- Use every opportunity to have conversations with your children.
- Turn off the car radio, the television, and the computers.

Tip #9
Encouraging Motivation and Engagement

Research shows that when people are happier, they are more productive. When companies invested more in employee support, their employee satisfaction rose, which translated into more profits…as much as triple.

Great companies like Apple, Disney, Starbucks, Southwest Airlines and Zappos create highly motivated employees who love where they work and motivate them to move mountains.

1. Forbes Magazine states a few ways to motivate and engage your employees to achieve is to provide a stable future, career advancement, and trustworthy leadership.
2. Think about what motivates them for the long term. Maybe it's flexible work hours or a flexible work location.
3. Employees also want a positive work environment. Make work fun.
4. Provide tools, training, support and sensitive understanding supervisors.
5. Practice random acts of kindness.
6. Act fairly. Give respect and create trust.

How Parents Can Increase Motivation & Engagement

- Motivation is what moves people to do what they do.
- Parents should motivate their children and increase their desire to learn.
- Build confidence by trying different fun activities to develop interest.
- Positive experiences build confidence and motivation while reducing anxiety.
- Teach your children they have control of their success by developing their skills
- Avoid comparing their progress to others.
- Learn to measure their success through their own efforts.
- Provide lots of encouragement and positive feedback.
- Act fairly. Give respect and create trust.

"If you do what you've always done, you'll get what you've always gotten."
- Tony Robbins

Tip #10
Showing Compassion

Compassion is showing a concern for others.

1. One way business owners can do this is by keeping their promises.
2. Give your employees what is important to them.
3. Provide feedback and support.

In the corporate community it is important that management shows compassion to their employees and demonstrates a commitment to their well-being. The good will that results from this demonstration of compassion only serves the overall success of the organization.

For example, several companies in Silicon Valley provide luxury bus shuttle services to their employees in the surrounding Bay Area. This benefits the employees by reducing stress and the environment by reducing carbon footprint.

Being a More Compassionate Parent

- As parents, avoid giving too many orders and being "the boss."
- Also avoid being a pushover and trying to make everyone happy.
- You send a message through your actions and non-actions.
- You also send a message through your reactions.
- Listen to what your family's wants and needs are and act accordingly.
- Stay focused on your family values, mission and vision.
- Discuss what each of you can give, create clear strategies and then take action.
- Ask for feedback.
- Adjust as needed to support the family.

"If you want others to be happy, practice compassion. If you want to be happy, practice compassion."
- Dalai Lama

Tip #11
Improving Emotional Intelligence

Webster dictionary defines emotional intelligence as the "skill in perceiving, understanding, and managing emotions and feelings." Highly emotionally intelligent leaders are aware of their emotions, how to manage it, how express it and are able to control negative inappropriate emotional outbursts. They know:

1. It increases the ability to handle conflict
2. It helps others do the same.
3. It increases awareness and relationships.
4. It decreases stress and anxiety.
5. It enhances relationships.
6. It has positive effects on decision-making skills and motivating others.
7. And positively effects the level of consciousness.

Highly emotionally intelligent leaders don't blame others for feeling angry, sad or any other emotions. The statement, "You made me so mad/angry/sad" is not in their vocabulary. They do know if they feel this way it is because of the "buttons" they created and they seek help to eliminate it instead of taking it out on others.

How to be Emotionally Intelligent Parents

- Demonstrate how your family should behave through your words and more importantly through your actions.
- Consistently positive and emotionally intelligent parents will earn the respect of their children.
- It's all about being able to control your emotions and being strategic about what emotions you allow to come out. This is especially important in the heat of the moment or at the time of an argument.

Before reacting....

- Breathe deeply three times.
- Take a step back and observe what is going on first.
- Look at the situation from a different perspective.
- Ask yourself what are the thoughts and feelings that run through your mind.
- Ask yourself what you are supposed to learn from this situation.
- Ask yourself how you can help the other person create a win-win situation.
- Now make a conscious choice to express and communicate appropriately AND at the appropriate time.

Tip #12
Listening Active

The importance of listening actively in corporate America cannot be understated. In environments where active listening takes place, all personnel are empowered in a leadership role. Active participation is encouraged and performance increases because employees are able to share their ideas and visions.

Listening actively can make or break a successful campaign and be the difference in millions of dollars. Listening actively:

1. Is removing all distractions.
2. Is listening to the speaker's signs and sounds.
3. Is feeding back that you have understood.
4. Allows the listener to really connect with the speaker and vice versa.
5. Is important because it helps you really understand the other person's perspective, concerns, ideas and needs.
6. Allows you to shift their energy and motivate them.
7. Offers greater clarity and empathy.
8. Brings in a higher level of awareness.
9. Is also how you learn and grow.

How to be a More Active Listener

- Pay attention to what your family members are saying, their tone of voice, energy levels, feelings and postures.
- Remember that facial expressions and breathing provides important clues to knowing the person's state of being.
- Notice what intuition comes up for you as the listener.
- Be especially compassionate towards each other as this is where unconditional love comes through and is received.
- It's also about what's NOT being said.
- It's hearing what is between the lines.
- Provide a safe environment where your children can express how they feel without fear or judgment.
- Create a nurturing environment where your children are encouraged to express themselves.

Ask open-ended questions, for example:

- How does that make you feel?
- What are your thoughts about that?
- What solutions can you think of?
- What's another way to look at that?
- What did you learn from that?
- What is stopping you?
- If you were to know, what would it be?
- Tell me more…

Tip #13
Forming Powerful Alliances

An alliance in business is a cooperative relationship between two or more companies to pursue a mutual benefit while maintaining their independence. This is all about synergy.

According to Napoleon Hill in his book **"Think and Grow Rich"** this is a "Master Mind" and is *"the basis of nearly every great fortune"* and that this *"principle holds the secret of the power"* for Carnegie, Ford, Edison, and Firestone.

The benefits are that:
1. Companies can learn necessary skills from each other.
2. Create a larger customer base.
3. Enhance and complement services and/or products.
4. Create visibility, credibility and probability.

A leader knows about delegating. They delegate to people within their alliance. These are people they can trust to accomplish the tasks in a timely manner. There is 100% accountability to ensure that everyone is on the page and will do what they say they will do. Bringing in people whose strengths compliment with yours.

How to Create Powerful Family Alliances

The way to create powerful alliances in the family is to take account of your strengths and weaknesses. It all starts with you. Know that you must lead by example and set the proper tone for the types of powerful alliances you want to create for your family.

> *"You are the average of the five people you spend the most time with."*
> **- Jim Rohn**

- The people your children spend time with will influence their choices, thoughts, beliefs, and eventually who they become.
- Take an assessment of who your family spends time with.
- Take an assessment of who your children spend time with.
- Ask yourself if these people elevate you or bring you down.
- Now make a conscious decision to promote, demote or terminate the relationship.

Tip #14
Tapping Into Intuition

Intuition is that "inner voice." It's the gut feeling and something instinctual that goes beyond logic. If we followed it, we just might be happier.

"Don't be trapped by dogma, which is living with the results of other people's thinking. Don't let the noise of others' opinions drown your own inner voice. And most importantly, have the courage to follow your heart and intuition."

- **Steve Jobs**

1. Richard Branson and Warren Buffet have credited intuition as leading them to greater success and higher profitability.
2. Successful business leaders use their intuition to take action because they know that is the SOURCE.
3. Successful leaders are not afraid of change. In fact, they often are the catalyst in instigating the change.
4. Successful leaders ask powerful questions to identify the best path forward.
5. They are able see opportunities in every situation.

How to Enhance Your Intuition for the Benefit of Your Family.

Everyone has some level of intuition. And with practice and focus you can become even more aware of things that you may not have been aware of in the past. As a parent, this will help you guide your family and children.

- Start with a meditation practice.
- There are plenty of samples on YouTube.
- An excellent goal is meditation for 20-minutes, twice a day.
- The key is start where you are now and do as much as you can do…even if it's only 5 minutes a day to start.
- Actively listen to your thoughts.
- Companies that are promoting on-the-job meditation: Apple, Google, Nike, Yahoo, HBO, and Navy SEAL.

Create affirmations to focus your mind. Here are samples:
- Money flows to me easily from expected and unexpected sources frequently.
- I attract and am blessed with loving, generous, and helpful people in my life.
- Learning is fun and exciting.
- I am awesome!!
- Use Google as a resource for finding more powerful affirmation for each member of the family.

Tip #15
Leading by Example

Like a chocolate fountain that starts from the top, it's crucial that leaders at the top of a company set the tone through their words and actions and define how employees should behave by being the model themselves first.

1. Victory is celebrated as a team.
2. Leaders take full responsibility. They do not point fingers. They own it!
3. Leaders lead by example. It's about talking the walk and walking the talk.
4. The leader does not yell or berate his or her team members.
5. This creates employee loyalty and commitment.
6. It gives the leader legitimacy.

"If your actions inspire others to dream more, learn more, do more and become more, you are a leader."
- John Quincy Adams

"You will get all you want in life, if you help enough other people get what they want."
- Zig Ziglar

Leading the Family by Example

As parents you are visible at all times. It's about showing up for your children at all times. That means going to their sports, academic, musical and other events. It's about them. It's about celebrating them. Do what you can to create a happy childhood for them.

- Your children are watching and emulating how you speak, act and react.
- Realize that you are a student and a teacher at all times. Be open to learning from your children.
- Ask your family for feedback on your behavior. Be willing to apologize and make a change for the better.
- Communicate with kind words and remember that hugs and smiles are free!
- Consistency is key in creating success and new habits. This will enable the family to blossom in wonderful ways.

"For things to change, first I must change."
                                    - Mahatma Gandhi

You've finished. Before you go…

Tweet/share that you finished this book.

Please star rate this book on Amazon.

Reviews are solid gold to writers. Please take a few minutes to give us some itty bitty feedback on this book and post it on line.

ABOUT THE AUTHOR

Jacqueline T. D. Huynh was born Trang-Dai Thi Huynh in Saigon, Vietnam and raised in Orange County, California. She is the first born of five girls. Her family arrived in the United Stated as refugees in 1975 with less than $20 in their pocket.

Jacqueline is a speaker, author, trainer and Certified Master in Neuro-Linguistic Programming (NLP), Leadership Development and in the Catharsis Application Program (CAP), which is a special program integrating art and music to release stress and negative emotions.

She helps business owners and families develop skills to become successful leaders in order to manifest their vision and leave a legacy.

She brings over 15 years of corporate and business world experience and integrates her coaching with her knowledge and life skills.

She found her inspiration, passion and purpose as a leadership coach after the suicide of her sister and her decision to leave her marriage. She desired to develop the skills and talents of a great leader and be a role model for her children.

She currently resides in the Los Angeles area with her 2 children. You can reach Jacqueline T. D. Huynh at:

www.IntegrativeMinds.com

**If You Liked This Book
You Might Also Enjoy…**

- **Your Amazing Itty Bitty® Parenting Teens Book** – Gretchen Downey

- **Your Amazing Itty Bitty® Communicating With Your Teenager Book** – Christine Alisa, MS

- **Your Amazing Itty Bitty® Marijuana Manual** – Kat Bohnsack

With many more Amazing Itty Bitty® Books available in paperback and online…

www.ingramcontent.com/pod-product-compliance
Lightning Source LLC
Chambersburg PA
CBHW061304040426
42444CB00010B/2511